"Children and adults will love these gentle, empowering books. The 'Learning to Get Along' series is a powerful tool for teaching children essential social skills such as empathy, respect, cooperation, and kindness. This straightforward and insightful series helps children visualize how their appropriate behavior positively impacts themselves and others. I heartily recommend this as a solid, classic resource for teaching affective skills to young children."

—Dr. Stephen R. Covey, Author, *The 7 Habits of Highly Effective People*

Respect and Take Care of Things

Cheri J. Meiners, M.Ed.
Illustrated by Meredith Johnson

free spirit
PUBLiSHiNG®

Helping kids
help themselves™
since 1983

Library of Congress Cataloging-in-Publication Data
Meiners, Cheri J., 1957–
   Respect and take care of things / by Cheri J. Meiners ; illustrated by Meredith Johnson.
     p. cm. — (Learning to get along)
  ISBN 1-57542-251-4
 1. Respect—Juvenile literature. 2. Caring—Juvenile literature. I. Johnson, Meredith. II. Title.
BJ1533.R4M45 2004
179'.9—dc22

                                 2004003184

Cover and interior design by Marieka Heinlen
Edited by Marjorie Lisovskis

10 9 8 7 6 5 4 3 2 1
Printed in Hong Kong

Free Spirit Publishing Inc.
217 Fifth Avenue North, Suite 200
Minneapolis, MN 55401-1299
(612) 338-2068
help4kids@freespirit.com
www.freespirit.com

Dedication

To Erika,
who enjoys creating
order and beauty

Acknowledgments

I wish to thank Meredith Johnson, whose charming illustrations resonate so well with the text, and Marieka Heinlen for the exuberant design. I appreciate Judy Galbraith and the entire Free Spirit family for their dedicated support of the series. I am especially grateful to Margie Lisovskis for her diplomatic style as well as her talented editing. I also recognize Mary Jane Weiss, Ph.D., for her expertise and gift in teaching social skills. Lastly, these books have been inspired by my children—especially Andrea, age six, as I have viewed life through her wise and innocent eyes.

I'm learning to take care of myself
and things around me.

I show respect
when I take care of things.

After I use something,
I put it where it belongs.

Everything has a place.

When I put things away,
the room looks neat. It feels comfortable.

And it's safe
when I keep things off the floor.

I can play with one thing at a time.

After I use something,
I can put it where it goes.

Then we'll all know where to find it.

8

I can help take care of things
I use with others and
things that someone
else used.

It can be fast and fun when we all help.

Some things need special care.

I can wash my hands
and use things gently.

That way they won't get dirty or broken.

I can use things a long time,

and use only what I need.

Things last longer when I don't waste.

I need to wait until I'm older
to use some things.

I can use other things safely
when I'm careful . . .

or when someone older helps me.

I can respect things around me, too.

Wherever I go,
I can leave things the way
I found them, or better.

When I pick up trash and litter,

I help keep places beautiful.

I can recycle, too.

I can use things again.
or in a new way.

People can trust me
to leave their things alone.

When I want to use something,
I can ask permission.

If the person says it's okay,
I'll be very careful.

I show respect for people
when I respect their things.

Some things are private—
just for one person.

I show that I'm responsible
when I leave those things alone.

I can take good care of things I use,
and respect all the things around me.

When I do,
everyone can enjoy them.

Ways to Reinforce the Ideas in *Respect and Take Care of Things*

As you read each page spread, ask children:

- What's happening in this picture?

Here are additional questions you might discuss:

Pages 1–9

- What are some things you can do for yourself?
- What do you do with the (blocks, dolls, trucks, puzzles) when you finish playing with them?
- What might happen if you don't put things away? if things are left on the floor? *(Discuss safety issues as well as the possibility of items being lost or broken.)*
- Have you ever lost something? How did you feel? What did you do to find it? How could you make sure not to lose it next time?
- What are things that you take care of at home? at school?
- What can you put away even if you weren't the one to use it?
- What is respect? *(You might explain respect by saying: "When you respect something, you show that you think it's important. You take good care of it.")*

Pages 10–13

- What are some things that are special to you? What do you do so they don't get dirty or broken?
- What are some things that you can use carefully, and not waste? *(examples: toothpaste, toilet paper, glue, paints)* How can you keep using things a long time? *(examples: repair a bike tire, tape a ripped page, put things away so they don't get lost)*

Pages 14–17

- What are some things that only grown-ups or older kids should use?
- What are things that you can use carefully so you and others stay safe? *(You may wish to discuss care needed in using things like electrical appliances, scissors, stairs, bathtubs, medicine, umbrellas, bikes, and skates.)*

Pages 18–23

- What can you do to leave a place better than you found it?
- What can you do if you have trash and don't see a place to put it?
- What do you think would happen if everyone littered? if nobody littered?
- What things can be recycled where we live? How can you help recycle?
- If you had some items that weren't needed, what could you do with them? *(Discuss community recycling of things like paper and bottles, recycling and reusing margarine tubs and plastic bags, selling or donating out-grown clothing, and so forth.)*

Pages 24–31

- What things do people have (at school, at home) that are just for them? *(examples: backpacks, coats, papers, diaries, purses, mail)* What can you do to respect other people's things?
- What can you do if you ask to use something and the person says no? *(examples: do something else, ask to use it later)*
- What are some things that belong to everyone? How can you take care of those things?

Other "Neat" Ideas

Storing Toys

- Keep "messy" toys out of reach so they can be used only when you're able to monitor.
- Keep other items in easily accessible places so children can become responsible for taking care of them.
- Keep items with small parts in containers with lids or in resealable plastic bags.
- Let children sort a large box of buttons—first by color, then by size, shape, and number of buttons. Encourage children to start their own collections of items such as coins, stamps, rocks, or leaves that they can sort, organize, and enjoy taking care of.

Tidying a Cluttered Room

- Use a timer and give a time frame: "Put things away for five minutes."
- Have children count items as they pick them up.
- Suggest picking up all of one item at a time: "First put away all the blocks, then all the crayons."

Staying Clutter-Free

- Show children where things go, and allow time for cleanup after every activity.
- Teach children to put one item away before using another.
- Temporarily put away items that children routinely neglect to pick up.
- Assign chores such as washing a sink, cleaning whiteboards, sorting clean socks, or picking up litter at a park to teach responsibility and a sense of community.

"Respecting Things" Games

Read this book often with your child or group of children. Once children are familiar with the book, refer to it when teachable moments arise involving positive behavior or problems related to taking care of things that belong to them or to others. Make it a point to notice and comment when children act responsibly. In addition, use the following activities to reinforce children's understanding of how to respect and take care of things.

Signs of Respect for Things

Discuss things children can do to take care of their own and other people's things. Have children choose and draw pictures of one thing they can do to respect and take care of something. Post the signs in places where they will be reminders. For example, display a picture of a child putting away toys near a toy box.

"Put It Away" Matching Game

Materials: Magazines, index cards, scissors, glue, drawing pencils or fine-point markers

Preparation: Cut out 6–12 pictures from magazines of items you want to encourage children to put away. Glue the pictures to index cards. Draw or cut out pictures to make cards with "where it belongs" pictures (storage places) that match each item. *(examples: coat/hook, book/shelf, milk/refrigerator, socks/drawer, backpack/cubby, pencil/pencil can, crumpled papers/wastebasket)*

Directions: Place the cards facedown randomly on the table or floor. The first player turns over two cards, seeking a matching item and storage place. If the cards are not a match, the child turns them back over. Play continues, with everyone trying to remember the location of the cards. After finding a match, a child may turn over two more cards. When all cards are matched, children look at their cards and choose an item that they will remember to put away during the week.

"Where Does It Belong?" Board Game

Materials: Sheet of cardstock at least 11" x 14", marker, magazines, index cards, scissors, glue

Preparation: Make a gameboard by drawing a 4" x 6" rectangle in the center of the cardstock. Divide the remaining space into four sections and mark these with names of rooms or areas at home or school. If you wish, cut out pictures of appropriate furnishings and glue them in the rooms. Make flash cards of household or classroom items by drawing or cutting and pasting several items onto index cards. Flash cards for a bedroom might include a pillow, shoes, pajamas, and a toy, while those for an art corner might include an easel, a paintbrush, drawing paper, and an apron. Prepare at least four items for each of the four rooms.

Directions: Place the cards facedown in the center of the gameboard. Have a child draw a card. Ask, "Where does that belong?" Then ask, "How should you take care of it?" or "What is the safe way to use this?" If appropriate, also ask, "Is this safe to use alone?" After answering appropriately, the child may place the card in the room where it belongs. Hold out cards with pictures of items that children aren't sure about and discuss their care and use after the game. Children take turns until all cards are gone.

Responsibility Role Plays

Preparation: On index cards, write individual scenarios similar to the following. Place the cards in a bag.

Sample Scenarios:

- Olivia left her bike out in the rain.
- After lunch, Pierre brought his plate and glass over to the sink.
- Ayanna made her bed when she got up in the morning.
- Jack couldn't find his shoes when it was time to go to school.
- Sofia played a game at school and left it on the floor.
- When Wilson got undressed, he put his dirty socks in the hamper.
- Luul hung her coat on a hook in the closet when she came home from school.
- Ramón's baby sister dumped his toys all over the floor, and Ramón put them back in the toy box.
- Hannah jumped on the couch when Mom was in the other room.
- Andrew hung up his towel after taking a bath.

Level 1

Have a child draw a card. Read or have a child read it aloud. Ask, "Is this showing respect for things?" or "Is this person taking good care of things?" When the answer is yes, help the child act out the scenario. Set "no" cards aside in a pile.

Level 2

Have a child draw a card from the "no" pile (Level 1). Read or have a child read the card and ask: "What do you think will happen next?" "What can this person do next time (to show respect for things)?" Help the child role-play the revised version of the scene.

"Everything in Its Place" Game

Materials: 8½" x 11" cardstock paper, markers, magazines, scissors, clear adhesive paper, tape, self-fastening fabric; *optional:* dolls or action figures

Directions: Assist children in drawing a picture of a classroom or bedroom. Use markers and magazine cutouts to make storage pieces (desks, cubbies, beds, baskets, bureaus) as well as small items that typically belong in a room. *Examples:* For a bedroom, children might draw and cut out clothes to put in a drawer or hamper or on a hook; for a classroom they might cut out pictures of toys to go on a shelf or in a basket. Cover the picture of the room and the other items with clear adhesive paper. Attach storage pieces like drawers and baskets to the drawing by taping them on three sides, leaving the top open like a pocket to hold the items to be stored. Use self-fastening fabric to attach items to other storage places like hooks and shelves. Make a game of having children (or their dolls and action figures) put "everything in its place."

More titles in Free Spirit's Learning to Get Along® series:

Our Learning to Get Along® series by Cheri J. Meiners, M.Ed., helps children learn, understand, and practice basic social and emotional skills. Real-life situations, lots of diversity, and concrete examples make these read-aloud books appropriate for childcare settings, schools, and the home. Each book: $10.95, 40 pp., color illust., S/C, 9" x 9", ages 4–8.

REACH OUT AND GIVE
Begins with the concept of gratitude; shows children contributing to their community in simple yet meaningful ways.

SHARE AND TAKE TURNS
Gives reasons to share; describes four ways to share; points out that children can also share their knowledge, creativity, and time.

TALK AND WORK IT OUT
Peaceful conflict resolution is simplified so children can learn to calm down, state the problem, listen, and think of and try solutions.

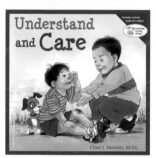

UNDERSTAND AND CARE
Builds empathy in children; guides them to show they care by listening to others and respecting their feelings.

LISTEN AND LEARN
Introduces and explains what listening means, why it's important to listen, and how to listen well.

JOIN IN AND PLAY
Teaches the basics of cooperation, getting along, making friends, and being a friend.

BE POLITE AND KIND
Introduces children to good manners and gracious behavior including saying "Please," "Thank you," "Excuse me," and "I'm sorry."

TRY AND STICK WITH IT
Introduces children to flexibilty, stick-to-it-iveness (perseverance), and the benefits of trying something new.

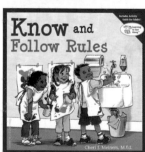

KNOW AND FOLLOW RULES
Shows children that following rules can help us stay safe, learn, be fair, get along, and instill a positive sense of pride.

WHEN I FEEL AFRAID
Helps children understand their fears; teaches simple coping skills; encourages children to talk with trusted adults about their fears.

ACCEPT AND VALUE EACH PERSON
Introduces diversity and related concepts: respecting differences, being inclusive, and appreciating people just the way they are.

To place an order or to request a free catalog of SELF-HELP FOR KIDS®
and SELF-HELP FOR TEENS® materials, please write, call, email, or visit our Web site:

Free Spirit Publishing Inc.
217 Fifth Avenue North • Suite 200 • Minneapolis, MN 55401 • toll-free 800.735.7323 • local 612.338.2068
fax 612.337.5050 • help4kids@freespirit.com • www.freespirit.com